For Girls!

Cool Creative

Deborah Chancellor

QED

Editor: Mandy Archer
Designer: Nikki Kenwood
Illustrator: Jessica Secheret

Picture credits
(t=top, b=bottom, l=left, r=right, c=centre, fc=front cover)
Shutterstock 4 blue67design and azzzya (spot art), 4t Ladyann, 4c Dmitry
Kolmakov and jocic, 4b Karkas, zhu difeng and Evgeny Tyzhinov 5tr tracie
andrews, cr clickthis, br aelitta, 5 asimjp (spot art), 6t Petro Feketa, 6tc
HomeStudio, 6c Dmitry Kolmakov, 6r Teeratas, 7t Ragnarock, 8b Ilike,
9cl Alena Ozerova, 9cr Matthew Cole, 10t Ramona Kaulitzki, upstudio
& malamalama, 10b Kiselev Andrey Valerevich, 11 Devor (spot art),
11b soloir, 12t Yuri Arcurs, 12c lanitta, 13t Olga Sapegina, 13b (annoyed
tween) Sparkling Moments Photography, 14b nuttakit, 15t Cheryl Casey,
15c Kiselev Andrey Valerevich, 15b M.antonis & kzww, 16c maximino,
16r Maksym Bondarchuk, 17t Anatema, 17cl Vojtech Beran, 18l elwynn,
18b Cosmin Munteanu, 19r Bluerain, 19b Aleksandar Mijatovic &
Monkey Business Images, 20b Marish, 21l Eduard Titov, 21r Jules Studio,
Beata Becla & Marilyn Volan, 21b terekhov igor, 22r iadams, 22b Felix
Mizioznikov, 23 vladislav_studio (spot art), 23b Melianiaka Kanstantsin,
24 rusalo4ka (spot art), 24c bikeriderlondon, 25t Nicola Kenwood, 26r
mixfree, 27r Mandy Godbehear, 27b Yuri Arcurs, 28 jagoda (spot art), 28bl
New Image, 28br pandapaw, 29cl Juriah Mosin, 29r Imageman

Be web wise! Neither the publishers not the author can be responsible
for the content of any websites that you visit or any third party websites.
Always check with an adult before going online and ask their permission
before registering any details on a new site.

Busy badges

Pin badges are a great way to stand out from the crowd. Most craft shops sell brilliant badge kits, or you could find some card, sticky-back plastic and safety pins, then have a go yourself.

Designer details

- ribbons
- fabric pens
- lace
- buttons
- brooches
- sequins and sew-on gems

Mix 'n' match

Customize old hair accessories to set off a brand-new outfit. Try sticking sparkly jewels on to hair clips, or sewing pretty coloured sequins onto a scrunchie. Trimmed scarves and ribbons look fab too.

Customizing kit

Before you throw anything away, see if there is any part of it that can be saved and stitched into something new. Keep buttons, patches and cute trims in a special bag – ready for you to rummage in next time you are feeling artistic.

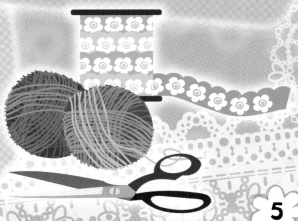

Bangles and boxes

Do you have trouble finding room for all your treasures and trinkets? Declutter your dressing table then make some cute new pieces to display!

Get personal

Make a feature out of personalizing your things – they'll be so much harder to lose! Use enamel paints to decorate a plain, plastic Alice band with your name, using all of your favourite colours.

Beauty box

Make a home for your hair accessories. Cover a shoe box with stickers and photos from glossy magazines. Cut up some thick card and fit it snugly inside the box to make sections for clips, Alice bands, ribbons and hair jewellery.

Treasure trove

If you fancy a trendy new jewellery box, just revamp your old one! Stick on some cool collage materials. Use strong craft glue, so that your decorations don't fall off.

Brilliant bangles

Bangles can take up loads of space in your jewellery box. Use nail polish to paint a blank CD holder in rainbow colours. Now you've got the perfect home for all your chunky wristbands!

Top 10 pretty things

1 holofoil paper
2 sweet wrappers
3 beads
4 fabric scraps
5 coins
6 shells
7 tassels
8 feathers
9 confetti
10 pressed flowers

Make Mum's day

Glass beads are fun to collect, and they also make beautiful necklaces and bracelets. Thread a matching set in your mum's favourite colours then present it to her as a gorgeous thank-you gift.

Special gift

If you want to make a special gift for your best buddy, try creating a paper bead necklace. Cut out thin triangular strips from colourful magazines, then tightly wind each strip around a drinking straw. Cover with clear glue and leave to dry, then cut up and thread!

Makeover madness

Is your bedroom lacking some va va voom? With a bit of effort and a few pots of paint, you can transform it into the perfect personal pad.

Make some space

It's hard to be creative if there is too much clutter around you. Set aside one Saturday to have a thorough clear-out, then take all your unwanted toys, books and clothes to a charity shop.

Colour change

Ask your mum or dad if you can paint your room a new colour. Think carefully about the shade you like – the colour will set the mood for the whole space.

All change

You can make your room seem bigger by moving furniture around. Draw a plan of your room, showing where you want everything to go. Check with your parents before you shift the big items.

Tidy up

If you've got loads of stuff, you'll need to find places to put it all. Grab some boxes and paint them in contrasting colours to your walls. Fill the boxes with your things and store them under your bed or desk.

Soft landing

Cushions and beanbags make your room extra comfy and create a relaxed atmosphere. Give your old cushions a makeover by sewing on pretty patches, or making funky fur covers.

Girls allowed!

Your bedroom's not complete without your own special door sign. Try designing one on your computer – make your name stand out with a funky font style. Now laminate your sign and hang it up!

Keep out!
Emma's room

Colours to match your mood

pink   cosy and comfy
blue   cool and quiet
lilac   relaxing and soothing
green   calm and peaceful
yellow   sunny and cheerful
orange   friendly and bold

Hot collections

Are you crazy about collecting? It's fun to build up a special box of treasures to show to your friends. Maybe you'll start a trend...

Collector club

Find out if there is a website or magazine that will tell you more about the kind of object you like to collect. The more that you learn, the bigger and better your collection will become.

Get this!

Want to start a new collection, but not sure what to go for? Here are some items that will look fantastic when displayed on any bedroom shelf.

- snow globes
- key-rings
- fridge magnets
- animal figurines
- costume dolls
- crystals
- fossils

On show

Don't hide your collection away! Ask an adult to put up some shelves for you. Make sure there will be enough space to display your collection, plus some room to spare as it grows!

Top trades

When you *begin* a sticker or card collection, check if some of your pals are collecting the *same thing*. That way, when you get doubles, you can arrange to do swaps.

In the album

A clever trading tip is to make up two albums. Use one for your collection, and the other for doubles. Keep your collection at home, and bring the doubles out with you to swap with friends.

Complete collection

If you manage to complete a whole series of cards or stickers, keep them safe in your album. One day, your collection will bring back happy memories and it may even be worth a fortune!

Secret diary

Do you write a diary, or are you thinking about starting one? Here are some secrets to help you create the most exciting journal ever!

Dear diary

Be realistic about the amount you can write. Find a time to write that works for you, when you're not too busy or tired. If you write in it at the same time each day, it will become a habit that you won't forget.

Book it in

Find a hardback notebook to write in. You could buy a diary with a lock, but take care not to lose the key or forget the combination. Customize the cover with patterns and doodles of your favourite things.

My Diary

What to write?

Write about the interesting stuff that happens to you and leave out all the boring bits. Don't go into detail about what you had for lunch or your lessons at school. Instead, dish out the day's juicy gossip and describe the funniest moments!

Hands off!

The most thrilling thing about your diary is keeping it secret. Keep an eye on any pesky brothers or sisters – don't let them get their hands on it!

Hiding places

Swap your hiding places around, but don't forget where you've put your diary for the next time you want to make an entry!

Good places
✔ behind your book shelf
✔ in your sock drawer
✔ under the mattress

Bad places
✘ in your bed
✘ in your school bag
✘ on your desk

Busted!

What if someone reads your diary? If you've written some upsetting stuff about them, say you are sorry, but remind the person that they shouldn't have read your private diary in the first place.

Clever codes

Try writing your diary in code, so no one else can read it. Remember how to crack your code, or you won't be able to understand all the brilliant stuff you've written afterwards!

3-shift cipher

Write out the alphabet, and then write it again in capital letters on the line below 3 spaces over. Your two lines should look like this:

a	b	c	d	e	f	g	h	i	j	k	l	m	n	o	p	q	r	s	t	u	v	w	x	y	z
X	Y	Z	A	B	C	D	E	F	G	H	I	J	K	L	M	N	O	P	Q	R	S	T	U	V	W

With this code, the alphabet gets shifted along by three spaces. You write 'X' instead of an 'a', 'Y' instead of a 'b' and so on. If you want to write 'bad', put down 'YXA'.

Fake names

Writing in code takes up lots of time. If you're in a hurry, then you could just write special names and places in code. Otherwise try choosing fake names for the people you are writing about.

Code message =
PQLM OBXAFKD
UV AFXOV!

Translated message =
Stop reading my diary!

Amazing anagrams

Disguise people's names by turning them into anagrams. Use the same letters, but put them in a different order. For example, the name 'Catherine' could become 'A rich teen'.

Back to basics

Write things backwards to confuse people who are trying to sneak a peek at your diary. 'Don't be nosy' looks much more baffling written as 'yson eb tnod'. Don't try this trick too often or it will be easy to spot.

Hidden messages

Hide the words you want to write in a sentence, so they only appear every sixth word. For example, '<u>My</u> Mum really loves my little <u>brother</u> when he says her perfume <u>smells</u> nice' hides the words '<u>My brother smells</u>'.

Invisible ink

Ever used invisible ink in your diary? Write something with a cotton wool bud dipped in lemon juice. To see what you have written, shine a bright torch on to the page.

Snap happy

Taking photos is great fun and it's so easy. You don't need a big expensive camera – just start clicking away with your mobile phone!

Camera crazy

If you're turning into a keen photographer, ask for a digital camera for your birthday or borrow one from your mum or dad. Take as many photos as you like, then delete the ones you don't want to keep.

Time to text

Text your photos to your mates to cheer them up or share a giggle. Sometimes the funniest pics are the out-takes – the ones that didn't turn out quite as you planned...

Photo opportunity

Many mobiles, hand-held game consoles and MP3s have cameras built into them. Learn how to use the photo function and practise taking pics at your next sleepover!

Look again

Think carefully about the kind of photos you enjoy snapping and keep an eye out for unusual subjects. Try capturing something ordinary from a brand-new angle.

Photo portfolio

- pretty portraits
- landscapes
- party pictures
- action shots
- animal magic
- city scenes

Photo booth

Meet your pals at the shops then pile into a photo booth – how many of you can fit in? Strike funny poses, then cut up the strip so everyone gets to take a picture home with them.

Save and send

Learn how to upload your photos onto a computer so that you avoid using up the memory disk on your phone or camera. Once you've got your pics stored on your computer, you can start emailing them to friends and family.

17

Smile!

Do you love taking photos, but sometimes feel disappointed with the results? Don't give up – there are all sorts of ways to improve your technique.

In the picture

Be careful how you frame your shot. If you are snapping people, don't stand too far away. For a great photo, think about what's close to you, as well as what's in the distance. Try turning your camera sideways to see if a vertical shot looks more interesting.

Ready, steady, go...

To take great action shots, use a camera with a fast shutter speed. If you don't want any blurring, you'll need to hold it perfectly still. It might help to fix the camera on to a mini-tripod.

Gotcha!

The best photo opportunities happen when you are least expecting them. Be ready, so if you see something you want to photograph, you won't miss it. Always have your camera handy!

Lights, camera, action!

Check that there's enough light to take your photo and make sure there are no shadows going over your subject. Look at the angle that the light is coming from, and don't face the sun when taking your shot.

How cute!

If you want to take animal photos, start with your pet. Take lots of pics so he or she gets used to the camera, then try to capture their personality with a few close-ups. You'll bag the best shots if you get down on their level.

Fab photo checklist

- ❑ Are you close enough to your subject?
- ❑ Have you sussed out what's in the background?
- ❑ Have you included all your subject in the frame?
- ❑ Do you need to use a flash?
- ❑ Do your fingers cover the lens?

Red eye

Do the people in your photos sometimes end up with glowing red eyes? This can happen when the flash shines into their eyes. Some computer programs can fix this problem before you print the photos out.

19

Photo gallery

Pictures are made for sharing – so don't hide them away! There are all kinds of creative ways to display the special moments that you've captured.

Photo board

Get a pin board for your room then put up photos of all your favourite people and animals. Add some silly speech bubbles to make your friends laugh! Change your montage as often as you wish.

Perfect present

Digital photo companies can print your shots on to anything from mugs to mouse mats. You could also use your pics to personalize a calendar for your family.

Photos dazzle ...
- as screen savers
- in collages
- on birthday cards
- in key-rings
- on the fridge
- in photo frames

Funky frames

Customized photo frames are perfect for those extra-special pictures. Add glamour to a plain wooden frame by sticking on feathers, glitter and sequins. Now it's ready to display a happy photo of you and all your friends!

Amazing albums

The best way to organize your pictures is to sort them into albums. It's easy to forget when and where you took a photo, so write a caption and date next to each one.

Simply the best?

If you've got stacks of similar photos, don't put them all together in your album – just choose the best of the bunch. You could slip in a few embarrassing out-takes for a laugh!

Protect your pics

Don't leave your photos in your phone or on your computer – if you upgrade you could lose them all. Print out your favourite pictures, then back them up by saving a copy on to a CD.

21

Super scrapbooks

Why not get creative and start scrapbooking? You'll get stunning results with just a few simple craft materials and a sprinkling of imagination!

Pick a theme

Choose a theme for a page in your scrapbook, such as your summer holiday. Collect photos, keepsakes and collage materials to go with your theme.

Time to choose

Crop the photos you want to use, or overlap them for a montage effect. Be selective, because you may only have room for one or two shots on a page.

Sticky business

Don't stick anything down until you are happy with the layout of your page. Use good craft glue that dries clear, and make sure that everything is well fixed. Don't shut the scrapbook until the glue is dry!

Cool collage

Lay out everything you want on the page, starting with the background material. Add layers of photos and mementoes to build up an eye-catching collage. Leave enough space to write some captions.

Caption time

Ask for help remembering interesting facts and stories to record in your scrapbook. Describe funny moments or write down special quotes. If you type your captions, pick interesting fonts and colours.

Essential scrapbooking kit

- ♡ Souvenirs and keepsakes
- ♡ Fabric scraps
- ♡ Coloured sheets of card
- ♡ Textured papers and tissue
- ♡ Pretty stickers
- ♡ Glitter
- ♡ Gel pens

Brilliant books

Now you've got the hang of scrapbooking, you've got the skills to create all sorts of wonderful journals that everyone will want to share.

Cover story

The front cover of your book should give you a taste of what's inside. Write the title in big decorative letters, then draw pictures around the edge or create a bright collage border.

Lucy Brown's Cheerleading Book

My first year at the All Stars!

Twelve top months

Find a large scrapbook, then create a fascinating record of the year according to you! Every month you could stick in seasonal photos, amazing news stories and souvenirs from the parties and days out that you enjoyed.

School days

Collect your best school pics, and save programmes and newsletters, too. Start a school scrapbook to share with your mates – it's funny to see how you have all changed during the year! Don't forget to write in everybody's names.

Coming home from hospital

Me aged 3

My 5th birthday

This is my life

Ask your family to dig out pictures of you as a baby, a toddler and as a little girl. Make a special album that's all about you, writing the age you were underneath each of the photos. Include lots of facts and stories, too.

Momentous milestones

⭐ First tooth
⭐ First steps
⭐ Riding a bike
⭐ First day at school
⭐ Birthdays
⭐ Christmas

Stencil it

Stencilling is a great way to decorate your scrapbooks. You can buy plastic stencils from craft shops, or ask an adult to cut your own design out of a thick sheet of card. Just lay your stencil down, then dab paint on it with a piece of sponge.

Keep it clean

When you've finished your scrapbook, take the time to carefully laminate the cover with sticky-back plastic. The plastic will stop it from getting marked or creased.

Gorgeous greetings

Home-made cards are so much better than shop-bought ones. A design by you shows how much you really care about your friends and family.

Getting started

Grab some felt-tipped pens and your art supplies, plus some rough paper for doodling. Sketch a few ideas out first, then transfer your favourite one onto a folded piece of white card. Colour in your design and stick on pretty decorations.

Inside and out!

Make sure your envelope looks stunning by covering it with flourishes and patterns. Try designing your own pretend postage stamp in the top corner! Inside the card use your best handwriting for the message.

Rhyme time

Why not compose a short poem to go inside your card? Try to make it rhyme if you can! Write the poem by hand, or type and print it so you can stick it in the right place.

Dear Amy,

The time has come to send to you
Special hugs and kisses, too.
This little card is just to say,

Have a super 10TH BIRTHDAY!

Jade xoxoxo

Pop-up surprise

Ask an adult to help you make a simple pop-up card using two sheets of paper. A pair of cut-out triangles folded back on the first sheet then pasted onto an outer sheet will look like a moving mouth when the card is opened up.

Pretty pad

You could use your craft materials to decorate other things, too! Why not customize a special notebook or diary? You could give it to your pal for her next birthday.

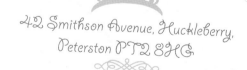

42 Smithson Avenue, Huckleberry, Peterston PT2 8HG

Neat notepaper

Design some personalized notepaper on your computer. Use a pretty font to type your address at the top of the page, then decorate the notepaper with some clip art.

Great gifts

Gifts you create yourself are special because they are completely unique! Each present is a designer one-off that is sure to be kept forever.

Mum's mirror

Make a special mirror for your mum. Cover the frame with a layer of soft clay, then press in seashells to make a pattern. It's the perfect way to use those shells you collected last summer!

Stuck on you

Why not make a fridge magnet for your grandparents? Get some polymer clay and a small magnet. Make a model of a cute animal, like a hedgehog, press the magnet underneath and leave it to set.

What a mug!

Get a plain white mug and paint on some funky stripes with enamel paints. If this is a gift for your dad, you could also personalize the mug with his name.

Daddy Monty

The sky's the limit

The Internet and your local library are both great sources for craft ideas. Birthdays are the ideal time to try out some brand new projects to give to your friends and family.

I want one of those!

- button brooch
- pot of paper flowers
- decorated trinket box
- jewelled bookmark
- papier maché mask

Tidy up!

Make your brother or sister a desk tidy. Cut some cardboard tubes to different lengths and fix them onto a small shoebox lid. Decorate the desk tidy with colourful acrylic paint.

Just charming

Design a phone charm for your best friend to remind her to call you! Buy some alphabet beads from a craft shop, threading them together to spell out her name.

Cool creative quiz

Are you smart about art? Find a sheet of paper and a pen, then work through this quiz to see how you rate in the arty stakes!

1. What's a cool way to deal with a hole in your jeans?
  a throw them away and get a new pair
  b cover the hole up with a funky patch
  c tear more holes to get a designer look

2. None of your clothes go together. What do you do?
  a wear them anyway and hope no one notices
  b swap some of your clothes with a friend
  c customize a few garments to make them match

3. Where do you store your bits and bobs?
  a in decorated boxes that match the colour of your room
  b stuffed under your bed or in a drawer
  c they just get thrown away

4. What do you do when you get bored with your bedroom?
  a put up with it – it's too much effort to change anything
  b swap rooms with your brother or sister
  c re-arrange the furniture and paint your room a new colour

5. How do you react when your pal starts a key-ring collection?
  a think about what you could collect, then start your own collection
  b copy her and start collecting key-rings too
  c tell her it's a silly idea

6. **What's the best way to start writing a diary?**
   a buy a pretty notebook
   b find a good time to write every day, so it becomes a habit
   c write an essay as your first entry

7. **How do you improve your photography skills?**
   a experiment with different techniques
   b blame your camera and give up
   c keep trying, but don't show anyone your pics

8. **What sort of card do you give your best friend for her birthday?**
   a a bought one, because life's too short to make one
   b you make a card, but you'll only give it if it looks 100 per cent professional
   c you make a card because it shows how much you care

Look back at these pages: New you (pages 4-5); Bangles and boxes (pages 6-7); Makeover madness (pages 8-9); Hot collections (pages 10-11); Secret diary (pages 12-13); Snap happy (pages 16-17); Smile! (pages 18-19); Gorgeous greetings (pages 26-27).

How well did you do?
Count your correct answers below to find out!

0-3 You like the idea of being creative, so do something arty today! It's well worth the effort.

4-6 You do have flair, but don't always make your ideas happen. Be more confident and your mistakes will turn into masterpieces!

7-8 You're bursting with creative ideas. Once you start, there's no stopping you!

Quiz answers: 1.b, 2.c, 3.a, 4.c, 5.a, 6.b, 7.a, 8.c.

Index